WORLD'S GREATEST

KID JOKES

The COMPLETE COLLECTION

OVER
350
FAMILY FRIENDLY
LAUGHS FOR ALL
OCCASIONS

13-Digit ISBN: 978-1-64643-179-3
10-Digit ISBN: 1-64643-179-0

This book may be ordered by mail from the publisher. Please include $5.99 for postage and handling. Please support your local bookseller first!

Books published by Cider Mill Press Book Publishers are available at special discounts for bulk purchases in the United States by corporations, institutions, and other organizations. For more information, please contact the publisher.

Applesauce Press is an imprint of
Cider Mill Press Book Publishers
"Where good books are ready for press"
501 Nelson Place
Nashville, Tennessee 37214

cidermillpress.com

Typography: Chelsea Market Pro

Printed in Malaysia

23 24 25 26 27 COS 6 5 4 3 2

WORLD'S GREATEST

KID JOKES

The COMPLETE COLLECTION

OVER
350

FAMILY FRIENDLY
LAUGHS FOR ALL
OCCASIONS

APPLESAUCE PRESS

Contents

CHAPTER ONE:

Medical Mayhem

Why did the clothesline go to the hospital?

It had a knot in its stomach.

What did the monster eat after the dentist filled his sore tooth?

THE DENTIST.

. . . .

Why did the sick shoe go to the cobbler?

IT WANTED TO BE HEELED.

Why are surgeons good comedians?

They always have their audience in stitches.

WHAT KIND OF BOAT DOES A DENTIST RIDE ON?

A tooth ferry.

Patient: Doc, you have to help me. I always feel like I'm on the outside looking in.

....

Psychiatrist: What kind of work do you do?

....

Patient: I'm a window cleaner.

NURSE: WHAT
SHOULD A PATIENT
DO WHEN HE'S
RUN DOWN?

DOCTOR: GET THE
LICENSE PLATE OF
THE CAR.

Girl: I wish the doctor would hurry up and see me. I'm only four years old.

· ·

Nurse: Be a little patient, dear.

· ·

Girl: I already am one!

Man: Doctor, my left ear feels hotter than my right ear. Is it an infection?

•••••••••••••••••••••••••

Doctor: No, your toupee is on crooked.

•••••••••••••••••••••••••

Mother: My son thinks he's a trash can.

•••••••••••••••••••••••••

Doctor: That's garbage.

Patient: Doc, am I really as ugly as people say I am?

· ·

Psychologist: Of course not.

· ·

Patient: Then why did you make me lie face down on your couch?

Where did the tin man go after he retired?

A rust home.

Patient: Help me, doctor! I just swallowed my harmonica.

~~~~~

Doctor: Luckily you don't play the piano.

Why did the actor end up at the hospital?

● ●

Everyone told him to break a leg.

Why did the miner go to a podiatrist?

● ●

He had coal feet.

Patient: Help me, doctor! I think I'm a bridge.

•••••••••••••••••••••••••

Doctor: My, my! What's come over you?

•••••••••••••••••••••••••

Patient: Two trucks and a minivan.

WHAT DOES A NURSE CALL A SUNBURN EMERGENCY?

Code Red.

Nurse: Now the patient thinks he's a door.

Psychologist: Maybe he'll finally start opening up.

What did the patient say to the clumsy dentist?

YOU'RE GETTING ON MY NERVES.

. . . .

What did Dr. Oz tell the sick Tin Man?

GO HOME AND GET
PLENTY OF BED RUST.

Man: Doctor,
I'm suffering
from insomnia.

• •

Doctor: That's a
tough one. Let me
sleep on it.

How did the nervous carpenter break his teeth?

He bit his nails.

JACK: DO YOU STILL HAVE A BAD CASE OF SUNBURN?

JILL: YES, BUT NOW I'M PEELING BETTER.

Patient: My hair is falling out. What can you give me to keep it in?

....

Doctor: How about a paper bag?

Man: Help me, Doc! My wife thinks she's a pretzel.

~~~~~~

Doctor: Bring her in and I'll straighten her out.

PATIENT: DOC, HOW DO YOU GET RID OF A PAIN IN THE NECK?

DOCTOR: TELL THEM TO LEAVE YOU ALONE.

Tim: I think you have bucket fever.

• •

Jim: Why do you think that?

• •

Tim: You look kind of pail.

Doctor: Your cough sounds better today.

~~~~~~

Boy: It should be. I practiced all night.

WHY DID THE EAGLE GO TO THE DOCTOR?

He had a soar throat.

WHY DID THE PIRATE TAKE HIS TRUNK TO THE DOCTOR?

It had a chest cold.

Father: How did you make out at the pie-eating contest?

• •

Boy: Not so good. My friend came in first and I came in sickened.

Did you hear about the dentist who treated a ghost?

They had a brush with the supernatural.

Why are there always openings at a dentist's office?

They're always looking to fill holes.

What did the arm bone say to the funny bone?

....

You're quite humerus.

Why did the window shade go to the psychologist?

....

It was up tight.

Why was the old house crying?

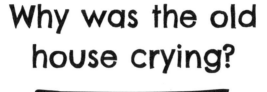

IT HAD WINDOWPANES.

What is a podiatrist's favorite TV game show?

HEEL OF FORTUNE.

WHY DO DENTISTS NEVER LIE?

They value the tooth at any cost.

Did you hear about the boy who wanted to be a dentist?

• •

He was enameled by the profession.

Why did the nice doctor go broke?

• •

He never thought ill of anyone.

PATIENT: DID YOU HEAR WHAT I TOLD YOU? I SAID I'M AS SICK AS A DOG!

DOCTOR: STOP BARKING AT ME AND SIT DOWN.

Why did the werewolf go to the psychologist?

He had a hair-raising experience.

Where do phlebotomists go to college?

IV LEAGUE SCHOOLS.

. . . .

What do you get if you cross a star and a podiatrist?

TWINKLE TOES.

Why did Santa Claus go to a psychologist?

Because he didn't believe in himself.

A lady went to see a psychologist. "Doctor," she said to him. "You have to help my husband. He just won the lottery and now all he does is worry about his money." The doctor comforted the lady. "There! There!" he said. "Calm yourself. Send your husband to me and after a few months of therapy he won't have that problem anymore."

Doctor: Where does it hurt, Mr. Cherry?

• •

Mr. Cherry: In the pit of my stomach.

Which doctor has the best voice?

• •

The choirpractor.

Why did the baby rocket go to the doctor?

• •

It was time for his booster.

What do you call a patient at a doctor's office?

• • • • • • • • • • • • • • • • • • • •

Someone sick and tired of waiting.

Why did the vampire take his son to the doctor?

• • • • • • • • • • • • • • • • • • •

He was eating necks to nothing.

Why did Frankenstein's monster go to the ER?

He was in shock.

WHY DID MR. & MRS.TURTLE TAKE THEIR SON TO A PSYCHOLOGIST?

They couldn't get their son to come out of his shell.

Boy: If you broke your arm in two places, what would you do?

• •

Girl: Stay out of those two places.

• •

Man: Every time I travel on a plane, I get sick. Doctor: It sounds like you have the flew.

Chester: How's your Aunt Charlotte?

• •

Lester: Her memory and her health are both failing her. She can't remember the last time she felt good.

WHY DO PRISON WARDENS CARRY FACE WASH?

It helps them prevent breakouts.

Patient: How can I cure my double vision quickly?

~~~~~~

Doctor: Shut one eye.

CHAPTER TWO:

Sports Snickers

What kind of cookies do baseball players eat in Maryland?

BALTIMORE OREOS.

• •

What do you call an invisible golf course?

THE MISSING LINKS.

What do you call
a photograph
of a baseball
thrower hanging
on the wall?

A pitcher framed.

Who is the laziest person in sports?

The coach potato.

RICK: DO YOU EVER TAKE AN ILLEGAL GOLF SHORTCUT?

NICK: NO. I ALWAYS PLAY THE FAIRWAY.

Nell: I'm a
White Sox fan.

•••••••••••••••••••••••••••

Dell: I'm a Red Sox fan.

•••••••••••••••••••••••••••

Mel: I'm a fan of
going barefoot.

What does a prizefighter
wear on a hot day?

● ● ● ● ● ● ● ● ● ● ● ● ● ● ● ● ● ● ● ●

Boxer shorts.

What does a golfer
who can't get a date
use to hit his ball?

● ● ● ● ● ● ● ● ● ● ● ● ● ● ● ● ● ● ● ●

A lonely hearts club.

Zack: I'm not much
of an athlete.

....

Mack: What do
you mean?

....

Zack: I got tennis
elbow playing golf.

What do you get if you cross a busy highway with a skateboard?

A trip to the hospital.

GOLFER: HAVE YOU NOTICED ANY IMPROVEMENT SINCE LAST YEAR?

CADDY: YES. YOU BOUGHT A NEW SET OF CLUBS.

Which country makes the best rods and reels?

• •

Poland.

Why did the cherry pull its car off the racetrack?

• •

It was time for a pit stop.

WHAT DID THE BOXER SAY TO THE PASSING TORNADO?

Can I go around with you?

Wife: Why do you have to play golf every Saturday?

• •

Husband: My doctor told me to take in more greens.

WHEN IS THE BEST TIME TO PLAY GOLF?

At fore o'clock.

What do poker players like to get in December?

CHRISTMAS CARDS.

. . . .

What does a winning NASCAR driver have?

WHEELS OF FORTUNE.

WHY DID THE EGG QUIT THE BASEBALL TEAM?

It couldn't crack the starting lineup.

Why did the baseball player stay inside?

• •

He was afraid of getting out.

Why did the football coach ask for 25 cents?

• •

He wanted a quarterback.

WHY DID THE DETECTIVE TAKE THE BASEBALL PLAYERS TO THE POLICE STATION?

To put them in his lineup.

WHY DID THE GOLFER CUT PART OF HIS SOCK?

He wanted a hole in one.

What did the salt cheerleaders do?

• •

They held a pepper rally.

Why did the golfer get a ticket?

• •

He was driving without a license.

How do pool players play poker?

● ● ● ● ● ● ● ● ● ● ● ● ● ● ● ● ● ● ● ●

They use cue cards.

What kind of boat did Babe Ruth own?

● ● ● ● ● ● ● ● ● ● ● ● ● ● ● ● ● ● ●

A dugout canoe.

What do you call a quick sketch of a New York baseball player?

A Yankee doodle.

Where did the baseball players' union stage a rally?

In the strike zone.

Why was Mr. Locomotive so proud?

•••••••••••••••••••••••

His son was a track star.

Why do basketball players spend so much time at home?

•••••••••••••••••••••••

Because they're not allowed to travel.

WHY DO SCARECROWS MAKE GREAT BASEBALL PLAYERS?

They're out standing in the field.

Why did the tennis player become a waiter?

He wanted to learn how to serve.

WHY DID THE NASCAR DRIVER BUY FOUR TOUPEES?

His car had bald tires.

Fran: Did you hear about the hairdresser who became a bodybuilder?

•••••••••••••••••••••••

Jan: No.

•••••••••••••••••••••••

Fran: Now she's curling iron.

What do you get if you cross a good poker player with a golfer?

THE ACE OF CLUBS.

• •

Why are fishermen great singers?

THEY KNOW A TUNA TWO.

What happened to the couch potato who tried to play quarterback?

HE GOT SACKED.

What did the driver say to the putter?

LET'S GO CLUBBING.

WHAT DO YOU CALL A HIGH SCHOOL GOLFER?

A student driver.

How do you light a fire under a lazy prizefighter?

Use a boxing match.

What do you call a funny bodybuilder?

. . . .

A he-he-man.

What did one street racer say to the other?

. . . .

This job is getting to be a real drag.

Did you hear about the golfer with car troubles?

His engine kept puttering out.

Which sports channel do vipers watch?

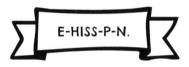

E-HISS-P-N.

. . . .

What is coffee's favorite hockey team?

THE BREWINS.

WHAT DID ONE GOLF CLUB SAY TO THE OTHER?

Let's go for a drive.

Why did the football player buy a feather mattress?

He wanted to touchdown.

What kind of tennis
did they play on
Noah's Ark?

DOUBLES.

• •

Why does the
boxer never silence
his phone?

HE LIKES THE RING.

What do you get when you don't refrigerate an athlete?

A spoiled sport.

What is a couch potato's best golf stroke?

• •

A chip shot.

How does a sprint runner take their coffee?

• •

With a dash of cream.

Why did the football lineman go to a psychologist?

He was having problems with a mental block.

WHEN DO BOXERS WEAR GLOVES?

When it's cold outside.

Dan: Did you hear about the hockey player who got a role in A Midsummer Night's Dream?

• •

Stan: No, who did he play?

• •

Dan: Puck.

Who invented the game of golf?

● ● ● ● ● ● ● ● ● ● ● ● ● ● ● ● ● ● ● ●

Our forefathers.

What did the baseball manager say to his new infielder?

● ● ● ● ● ● ● ● ● ● ● ● ● ● ● ● ● ● ● ●

If at first you don't succeed, we'll try you at second or third base.

What casts spells and plays croquet?

A WICKET WITCH.

. . . .

What did the baseball pitcher put on the floors of his house?

THROW RUGS.

WHY DIDN'T THE OLYMPIC DIVER RUN FOR POLITICAL OFFICE?

He had no platform.

What do you get when surfers riot?

A BEACH BRAWL.

· ·

Where do small onions play baseball?

IN THE LITTLE LEEKS.

WHAT DOES A LIBRARIAN PLAY GOLF WITH?

A book club.

Why did the salesman play baseball?

He wanted to work on his pitch.

WHAT DO YOU GET WHEN YOU CROSS A GOLFER AND A NASCAR DRIVER?

Someone who likes driving in circles all day long.

Where did the judge play on the court softball team?

Nowhere. The judge was on the bench.

ATTENTION:
Is a bad golfer a bogeyman?

WHY DID THE GIANT AIR CONDITIONER GO TO A BASEBALL GAME?

He was the world's biggest fan.

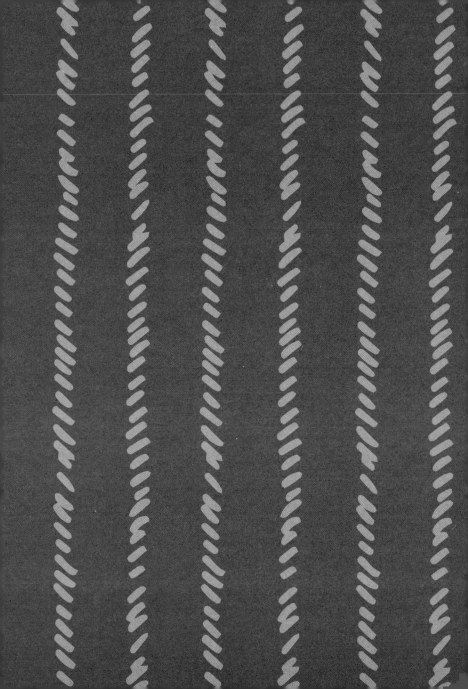

CHAPTER THREE:

Family Fun

MILLIE: IS THAT
MRS. MARGARINE'S
HUSBAND?

TILLIE: NO. IT'S HER
BUTTER-IN-LAW.

Son: Dad, can you tell me what a solar eclipse is?

Father: No sun.

· ·

Father: The new baby looks just like me.

Aunt: That doesn't matter as long as he's healthy.

Husband: Why are you knitting three socks?

• •

Wife: Our daughter said her new baby has grown a foot since we last saw him.

What did the bedroom say to the sloppy teenager?

• •

Here's another fine mess you've gotten me into.

What do werewolves read to their children at bedtime?

• •

Furry tail stories.

Mother: Don't swim on
a full stomach.

• •

Son: Okay, Mom. I'll do
the backstroke.

WHAT DID THE TIDY MOM TELL HER SLOPPY KIDS?

Quit messing around the house.

MY SISTER BET I
COULDN'T MAKE
A CAR OUT OF
SPAGHETTI.

You should have seen her
face when I drove pasta.

What do you call a priest that becomes a lawyer?

A FATHER IN LAW.

• •

What do you call it when your sister watches a sad movie?

A CRY SIS.

Patient: Can you cure me, doctor?

....

Doctor: I'm afraid not. Your illness is hereditary.

....

Patient: In that case, send the bill to my parents.

Joey: When my grandpa
sneezes, he always puts
his hand over his mouth.

• •

Zoey: To stop germs
from spreading?

• •

Joey: No, to catch
his teeth.

What do you call two siblings who take your money?

FINE BROTHERS.

• •

My sister, my aunt, and my mother all have holes in their tights.

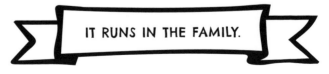

IT RUNS IN THE FAMILY.

Son: Can I go out
tonight?

. . . .

Father: With so much
homework?

. . . .

Son: No, with my
girlfriend.

Don: My parents got mad at me for talking about ducks.

••••••••••••••••••••••••

Juan: What? Why?

••••••••••••••••••••••••

Don: They told me not to use fowl language.

Father: Stop misbehaving and I'll tell you the joke about the big Christmas present.

••••••••••••••••••••••

Boy: And if I don't stop misbehaving?

••••••••••••••••••••••

Father: Then you won't get it.

KEN: MY UNCLE
IS NOW WITH
THE FBI.

LEN: I KNEW
THEY'D CATCH UP
WITH HIM SOONER
OR LATER.

Son: When I grow up, I want to drive a steamroller.

• •

Father: Well in that case, son, I won't stand in your way.

Chester: I heard your sister married a second lieutenant.

~~~~~~~

Lester: Yeah. The first one got away.

Little Boy: Mom! I spilled a six-pack of soda all over the stovetop.

• •

Mom: Oh great! Foam on the range.

UNCLE AL: I KNOW I'M UGLY. LAST CHRISTMAS MY PARENTS GAVE ME A TURTLENECK SWEATER THAT HAD NO HOLE FOR MY HEAD.

What did the mom fire
say to the dad fire?

• •

I'm so proud of arson.

Did you hear about
the former straight-A
student who got
in trouble with his
parents?

• •

Looks like he was stung by a B.

What did Santa Claus get when he filed for a divorce?

An independent Claus.

Mother: All right, who put dirty fingerprints all over the newly painted wall? Was it Matthew or Marty?"

• •

Marty: It was Matthew, Mom. I saw him at the scene of the grime.

Dora: We named our son after English royalty.

●●●●●●●●●●●●●●●●●●●●●●●●

Nora: Really? What do you call him?

●●●●●●●●●●●●●●●●●●●●●●●●

Dora: The Prince of Wails.

Why did the daydreamer disobey his parents?

It kept him grounded.

My parents warned me about procrastination.

• •

I told them, "Just you wait."

Why do doctors make good parents?

• •

They have plenty of patients.

ANNE: HOW MANY RELATIVES WERE AT YOUR FAMILY PICNIC?

JAN: THERE WERE SIX UNCLES AND ABOUT A MILLION ANTS.

Teenage Girl: What a beautiful car. Let's go buy it.

~~~~~

Father: Right. Let's go right by it.

Aunt: Don't children brighten up a home?

● ● ● ● ● ● ● ● ● ● ● ● ● ● ● ● ● ● ● ●

Father: Absolutely! They never turn off any lights.

Jack: My uncle cleaned
up on Wall Street.

••••••••••••••••••••••

Mack: Is he an investor?

••••••••••••••••••••••••

Jack: No. A janitor.

Cabin Boy #1: My grandfather dug the Panama Canal.

. . . .

Cabin Boy #2: Big deal. My uncle killed the Dead Sea.

Father: Do you want me to help you swing that baseball bat, son?

● ●

Boy: No Dad. It's time for me to strike out on my own.

Jill: My father makes
sofas all day.

• •

Bill: What does he do
when he comes home?

• •

Jill: He sleeps on his job.

What did Mr. and Mrs. Drum name their twin sons?

• •

Tom-Tom.

What did the mom printer say to the daughter printer?

• •

Don't speak to me in
that tone of voice!

Kelly: I decided to cook a big surprise dinner for my family the other night.

• • • • • • • • • • • • • • • • • • • •

Nelly: They must have been so surprised!

• • • • • • • • • • • • • • • • • • • •

Kelly: They would have been, if the fire trucks hadn't given it away.

Mother: Billy! Stop reaching across the dinner table. Don't you have a tongue?

• •

Billy: Yes, Mom, but my arms are longer.

"Donna, what happened
to our pet canary?"
a mother asked her
daughter. "The cage
is empty. The bird
is gone." "Hmm,"
answered the little girl.
"That's funny. It was
there a minute ago
when I vacuumed out
its cage."

MY PARENTS
WON'T SAY
WHICH OF THEIR
SIX KIDS THEY
LOVE THE BEST,
BUT THEY TOLD
ME I FINISHED
JUST OUT OF THE
TOP FIVE.

Mom: Billy! Why didn't you answer me?

....

Billy: I did. I shook my head.

....

Mom: Well did you expect me to hear it rattle all the way upstairs?

WHAT DID THE CALF SAY TO THE SILO?

Is my fodder in there?

Ted: How old is your great-grandfather?

● ●

Jed: I'm not sure, but he must be pretty old. His social security number is one.

Tina: My son came to visit for summer vacation.

• •

Deana: How nice! Did you meet him at the airport?

• •

Tina: Oh, no. I've known him for years!

WHAT DO YOU CALL A FISH'S DAD?

The cod father.

Did you hear about the dad who bought his son a fridge for Christmas?

He couldn't wait to see his son's face light up when he opened it.

What kind of music should you listen to on Father's Day?

....

Pop music.

Did you hear about the cable company that's going to have a baby?

....

They're expecting a bundle of joy.

CHAPTER FOUR:

Nifty Knock-Knocks

Knock! Knock!

Who's there?

Weight.

Weight who?

Weight a minute
and I'll tell you.

Knock! Knock!

Who's there?

Seldom.

Seldom who?

I'm here to seldom
cookies.

Knock! Knock!

Who's there?
Marsha.
Marsha who?
Marsha mellow.

....

Knock! Knock!

Who's there?
Glow.
Glow who?
Glow ahead punk.
Make my day.

....

Knock! Knock!

Who's there?

Scott.

Scott who?

Scott to be 10 degrees
outside, open the door!

Knock! Knock!

Who's there?

Ima.

Ima who?

Ima coming in,
are you decent?

Knock! Knock!

Who's there?

Mums.

Mums who?

Mums the word,
so be quiet.

Knock! Knock!

Who's there?

Polk.

Polk who?

Polk your head out
and take a look.

Knock! Knock!

Who's there?
I Otis.

I Otis who?
I Otis dollar to
your father.

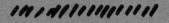

Knock! Knock!

Who's there?

Mark.

Mark who?

Mark this date on
your calendar.

Knock! Knock!

Who's there?

Daren.

Daren who?

Daren back again!

....

Knock! Knock!

Who's there?
Hugh Paine.
Hugh Paine who?
Hugh Paine in the neck.

....

Knock! Knock!

Who's there?

Abby.

Abby who?

Abby is trying to sting me, let me in!

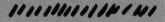

Knock! Knock!

Who's there?

Athena.

Athena who?

I know Athena two
about doors!

Knock! Knock!

Who's there?

Harve.

Harve who?

Harve your tickets
ready.

Knock! Knock!

Who's there?

Nicholas.

Nicholas who?

Nicholas, penniless,
and broke.

Knock! Knock!

Who's there?
Hood.
Hood who?
Hood you care
to let me in?

Knock! Knock!

Who's there?

I. Lois.

I. Lois who?

I. Lois my way.
Can you help me?

Knock! Knock!

Who's there?

I lecture.

I lecture who?

I lecture dog out
when I came in.

Knock! Knock!

Who's there?
Tattle.
Tattle who?
Tattle be the day
when I tell you.

Knock! Knock!

Who's there?

Auntie.

Auntie Who?

Auntie-histimine.

Knock! Knock!

Who's there?
Hula.
Hula who?
Hula-la! It's a
beautiful day.

Knock! Knock!

Who's there?

Ty.

Ty who?

Typhoon.

~~~~~~~

Knock! Knock!

Who's there?

Chair.

Chair who?

Chair with those
around you.

Knock! Knock!

Who's there?

Muffin.

Muffin who?

Muffin ventured,
muffin gained.

Knock! Knock!

Who's there?
Stirrup.
Stirrup who?
Stirrup the lemonade.

Knock! Knock!

Who's there?

Peace.

Peace who?

Peace open the door.

•••••••••••

Knock! Knock!

Who's there?
Bizet.
Bizet who?
Bizet me at my house
next weekend.

•••••••••••

Knock! Knock!

Who's there?
It's Max.
It's Max who?
It's Max no
difference to me.

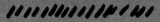

Knock! Knock!

Who's there?

Frame.

Frame who?

Frame and fortune
await on your doorstep.

~~~~~~

Knock! Knock!

Who's there?

Pig.

Pig who?

Pig me up at
two o'clock.

Knock! Knock!

Who's there?

Hits.

Hits who?

Hits later than
you think.

Knock! Knock!

Who's there?
Marie.
Marie who?
Marie thon.

Knock! Knock!

Who's there?

Hiam.

Hiam who?

Hiam here for a visit.

Knock! Knock!

Who's there?

Hardy.

Hardy who?

Hardy har har! The joke is over. Let us in.

Knock! Knock!

Who's there?
Nobel.
Nobel who?
Nobel so I knocked
instead.

~~~~~~

Knock! Knock!

Who's there?

Kent.

Kent who?

Kent you see who I am?

Knock! Knock!

Who's there?

Freeze.

Freeze who?

Freeze a jolly good
fellow, which nobody
can deny.

Knock! Knock!

· · · · · · · · · · · ·

Who's there?
Hoffa.
Hoffa who?
Hoffa is it to the
next gas station?

· · · · · · · · · · · ·

Knock! Knock!

Who's there?

Quint.

Quint who?

Quint fooling around
and open the door.

Knock! Knock!

Who's there?

Closure.

Closure who?

Closure mouth and
open the door.

~~~~~~~

Knock! Knock!

Who's there?

Toby.

Toby who?

Toby or not Toby,
that is the question.

CHAPTER FIVE:

Funny Things

What happened when the sink and the bathtub started an advertising campaign?

● ● ● ● ● ● ● ● ● ● ● ● ● ● ● ● ● ● ● ●

They plugged themselves.

What did the clothesline say to the wet laundry?

● ● ● ● ● ● ● ● ● ● ● ● ● ● ● ● ● ● ● ●

You're really dampening the mood.

WHAT DID ONE SPEAKER SYSTEM SAY TO THE OTHER?

I have some sound advice for you.

Why did the parked clock get a ticket?

IT WAS OVER THE TIME LIMIT.

• •

What did the nose say to the index finger?

STOP PICKING ON ME.

What's the best way to ship someone a toupee?

Send it via hairmail.

WHAT DID THE GUITAR SAY TO THE ROCK MUSICIANS?

Pick me.

WHY WAS THE ARROW SO ANGRY?

It was fired from a crossbow.

Why did the mattress go to the doctor?

It had spring fever.

What does a novel wear to keep warm?

A dust jacket.

MAN: DOES YOUR
WRISTWATCH
KEEP ACCURATE
TIME?

JOGGER: NO, IT
RUNS FAST.

What do you get when a phone wears a shirt?

• •

A ring around the collar.

What did the broken clock say?

• •

Will someone please
give me a hand?

WHY WAS THE LETTER DELIVERED IN THE MORNING ALL WET?

It had postage dew.

WHAT DID ONE BICYCLE WHEEL SAY TO THE OTHER?

Was it you who spoke to me?

WHEN DO OLD CLOCKS PASS AWAY?

When their number is up.

WHAT DID ONE HELICOPTER SAY TO THE OTHER?

Drop by my pad later today.

WHAT DID THE SHARPENER SAY TO THE PENCIL?

You can leave now.
You've made your point.

~~~~~~

What did the sword say to the angry saber?

Don't get all bent out of shape.

~~~~~~

Publisher: Is this book about blankets any good?

••••••••••••••••••••••••

Editor: It's just another cover story.

Why did the broken chair lose an argument?

It didn't have a leg to stand on.

What do you get if you cross the ocean and a cartoon duck?

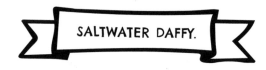

SALTWATER DAFFY.

· ·

What kind of dots dance?

POLKA DOTS.

WHAT DID THE CLOTHESLINE SAY TO THE CLEAN LAUNDRY?

Hey guys! Hang around with me for a while.

What language do clocks speak?

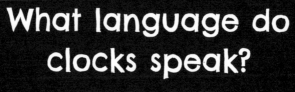

TICK TALK.

• •

What did the old lawn chair say to the new lawn chair?

WELCOME TO THE FOLD.

WHAT DID THE GAS OVEN SAY TO THE FURNACE?

You've really got me fuming.

What did one cemetery say to the other?

Are you plotting against me?

Jenny: Did you hear
the rumor about the
burning building?

• •

Penny: No. Is it
hot gossip?

Why did the trumpet take an algebra class?

It wanted to be a math tooter.

What do you get if you cross a diaper and a handbag?

A CHANGE PURSE.

. . . .

What did the cowboy say to the tangled lasso?

THAT'S KNOT FUNNY.

What should you do if your clothes keep getting wet?

Dry harder.

Did you hear about the entertainment center that wouldn't sit down?

It was a T V stand.

WHY DID THE READING GLASSES HATE TRAVELING?

They weren't good with distance.

What did the fast car
say to the sharp curve?

● ●

It was an honor to swerve you.

What do you get when
you cross a purse with
a dark room?

● ●

I don't know, but you'll never
find anything in there!

Why are rich Englishmen so strong?

•••••••••••••••••••••••

All their money is
measured in pounds.

What did the ceiling say
to the chandelier?

••••••••••••••••••••••••

You're the only bright spot in my life.

WHY DID THE PLAYING CARD BECOME A SHIP?

It wanted to be a full deck.

Hal: What do you call a boomerang that doesn't work?

Val: A stick.

A man built a car
totally out of wood.
It had wooden seats,
a wooden body and
wooden wheels. It
even had a wooden
engine. There was only
one big problem with
his invention: the car
wooden go.

What did the drumstick say to the drum?

I bet I can beat you in a race!

Did you hear about the percussionist running for office?

He's working on drumming up support.

WHY WAS THE WINDOW WORRIED?

He thought he was going blind.

What did the handyman say to the wall?

One more crack like that
and I'll plaster you.

WHY DID THE PARACHUTE SCHOOL CLOSE?

It had too many dropouts.

What did Mr. Candle say to Ms. Candle?

Are you going out tonight?

Why did the little boy pull the plug on the bathtub?

· ·

He wanted to go for a drain ride.

What does Santa call where he lives?

· ·

His ho-ho-home.

WHY WAS THE SINK SO TIRED?

It was feeling drained.

WHY DID THE BULLETIN BOARD QUIT HIS JOB?

He just couldn't tack
it anymore.

Reporter: I had to leave that new play early. Did it have a happy ending?

• •

Critic: We were all happy when it was over.

WHAT COLLEGE DID MR. CLOCK GRADUATE FROM?

Georgia Tick.

What did one cabinet say to the other?

Help your shelf.

WHY DID THE SHOE SAY OUCH?

It bit its tongue.

Why are everybody's pants too short?

•••••••••••••••••••••••

Because their legs always
stick out two feet.

Why did the wheel get
an education?

•••••••••••••••••••••••

Because it wanted to
be well-rounded.

Cowgirl: Do you want to hear a joke about a cattle roundup?

•••••••••••••••••••••••

Cowboy: No thanks. When you've herd one, you've herd them all.

Which state is the trouser state?

PANTSYLVANIA.

. . . .

Which state is very cold in the winter?

BURRMONT.

Which state is kind of sloppy?

Messachusetts.

Which state has the most highways?

Road Island.

What do you get if you cross a traffic light and a bonfire?

SMOKE SIGNALS.

. . . .

What is full of holes but still holds water?

A SPONGE.

WHY DID THE CHEF PUT A CLOCK IN A HOT PAN?

He wanted to see time fry.

CHAPTER SIX:

The Daffy Dictionary

Acorn:
An oak in a nutshell.

Acquaintance:
A person you know well enough to borrow from but not well enough to lend to.

Actor:
A person who works hard at being someone other than himself most of the time.

Adult:
A person who has stopped growing at both ends and is now growing in the middle.

• • • • • • • • • • • • •

Air Force Pilots:
Soldiers with their noses up in the air.

Alarm clock:
A device to wake up people
who don't have small children or
pets that need to go out.

Antarctic:
Snowman's land.

Antiques:
Merchandise sold for old time's sake.

Archaeologist:
Someone who keeps digging old things up.

Authorship:
A writer's canoe.

Baby quadruplets:
Four crying out loud.

Bad driver:
The person your car rear-ended.

Balloon:
Air today, gone tomorrow.

Bandstand:
What a band has to do when
someone takes away their chairs.

Baseball's Minor Leagues:
The hope diamonds.

Basketball:
A fancy dance for bugs held in a basket.

Big Belly Laugh:
Girth quake.

Birth announcement:
A stork quotation.

• • • • • • • • • • • •

Blister:
A heel's revenge for
being stepped on.

• • • • • • • • • • • •

Bore:
A pig that's not very entertaining.

Bread:
Raw toast.

Broke:
Something that takes more
money than you have to fix.

Bus Operator:
A person who drives away
even his best customers.

Business:
When you don't have any
of it, you go out of it.

Buzz saw:
A honey of a woodcutter.

Camel:
A horse with a speed bump.

Carp:
A musical instrument played
by angelfish in heaven.

///////////////////

Caterpillar:
An upholstered worm.

/////////////////////

Change purses:
Old money bags.

Character:

A thing few people have
and a lot of people are.

College:

A place where a lot of
wise guys hang out.

Computer crash:

When electronics byte the big one.

Cookout:
A chef on strike.

Cottontail:
A hoppy ending.

Cowardice:
Cold water when it gets scared.

Cricket:

A game played by English grasshoppers.

Critic:

A person who loves to hate plays and movies.

Declaration of Independence:
A doctor's excuse that allows you to miss school for a week.

• • • • • • • • • • • •

Dentist:
A doctor with a lot of pull.

Diet:
The victory of mind over platter.

Diplomacy:
Saying nice things to and
doing nice things for people
you really can't stand.

Duck:
A chicken with flat feet.

Dust:
Mud with the juice squeezed out.

Egotist:
An I-for-an-I kind of guy.

Encore:
Using flattery to get more
than you paid for.

Fast food:
an oxymoron.

Fish:
A creature that goes on vacation the same time most fishermen do.

Flagon:
A patriotic dragon.

Fresh water:
You used to get it by turning on a tap, now you get it by twisting off a cap.

Friend:
A person who dislikes the same people you do and also has the same enemies.

Funeral home:
Where people are dying to get in.

• • • • • • • • • • • •

Garlic:
Exercise food to make
your breath strong.

• • • • • • • • • • • •

Gigantic:
An antic performed by
a wise guy giant.

Glove:
A sock you wear on your hand.

Good Manners:
The noises you don't make
while eating or drinking.

Good sport:
A foe that always lets you have the
first pick when selecting teams.

Grand Canyon:
America's Hole of Fame.

Granny Knot:
What happens when Granny
forgets to put her glasses on
and ties her shoelaces.

Gripe:
A ripe grape.

Hair:
A dome covering.

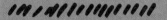

Halloween:
Pranksgiving time.

Harmonica:
Sweet chin music.

Hibernate:
To live on burrowed time.

Hijack:
A tool for changing tires
on an airplane.

Honesty:
The bitterest of drinks to swallow.

Horse sense:
Stable thinking.

Hospital:
Where the idea of visiting one is enough to make you sick.

Huddle:
Athletes getting together to play some football.

Hug:
People pulling together.

Manager:
The only thing they manage
is to get on your nerves.

On sale:
Buy twice as much for half the guilt.

Patients:
The more there are of them,
the less of it you have.

. . . .

Purse:
Something that, the smaller it is,
the more stuff you have in it.

. . . .

Raising a child:
A teen building exercise.

Restaurant:
Where you pay more to eat less.

Shoes:
Something to ensure de feet.

Sleep:
The one thing you can
never get enough of.

Tailor:
Someone always on
pins and needles.

////////////////

Taxi Driver:
Someone who gets in trouble
for going the extra mile.

////////////////

Thermostat:
The higher it goes,
the lower you feel.

ABOUT APPLESAUCE PRESS

Good ideas ripen with time. From seed to harvest, Applesauce Press crafts books with beautiful designs, creative formats, and kid-friendly information on a variety of fascinating topics. Like our parent company, Cider Mill Press Book Publishers, our press bears fruit twice a year, publishing a new crop of titles each spring and fall.

"Where good books are ready for press"
501 Nelson Place
Nashville, Tennessee 37214

cidermillpress.com